SURV

P.E.

by John McClelland
Illustrated by Rob Gordon

HENDERSON
P U B L I S H I N G   P L C

Are you keen on P.E.? Or do you run a mile to escape games at school? Well, the S.A.S. ground rules just might surprise you ...

"It is not winning that is important but it is taking part which counts..." That's what everyone says about sport. Everyone, that is, except the P.E. Teacher! To this sports fanatic, what really counts is winning cups, badges and medals for your school. Then he can show them off on Parents' Evening and take all the credit even though it was you who did the work.

"Playing sports will make a man of you..." Fine for the lads, maybe, but what about the girls? Don't worry, girls - sports are just as likely to turn you into a flat-nosed gorilla with cauliflower ears, chipped teeth and a pair of legs that an elephant could be proud of.

"Never mind, dear, it doesn't matter if you don't get picked for the team..." Mum or dad might *say* that, but don't you believe it! When the trials start, there's dad bellowing instructions at you through a megaphone, and mum's arguing with the other parents about whose child is best.

You *better* get picked for the team ...

'Physical jerks' is another term for exercise... or is it? Physical jerks are also certain *people*. You know the ones - too many muscles, chests like cow's stomachs, brains the size of peas - you can spot them running along the road in shiny shorts, woolly hats and fingerless gloves on a wet Saturday afternoon when any normal jerk would be lying on the sofa, feet up, watching other physical jerks on the telly. Now wouldn't they?

At school, you may have noticed one thing - all teachers think they are experts. Is your games teacher one of those? Then you're bound to be treated to their 'expert' views on every sport ever invented. But if only you could dig out that teacher's old School Reports, they would probably read something like this...

SCHOOL REPORT

P.E.   Jones has managed to do half a press-up this term which is a great improvement on his previous best.

Basketball   Jones has been asked to stop playing next year. Perhaps basket weaving would suit him better.

Rugby	Jones has finally found a position which suits him and will be playing as the ball next term.
Judo	Jones breaks into tears if anybody in a white suit comes anywhere near him.
Gymnastics	Jones refuses to try the beam without a safety net and a parachute.

AWFUL ATHLETICS

Athletics is for athletes but suddenly, on Sports Day, everyone is expected to take part, even if they have two left feet and can't outrun a snail!

It's bad enough coming last in every race and doing a long jump that a frog would laugh at, without your parents there to watch. Even worse, they will probably take part in the Mother's and Father's Races. As you watch them huffing and puffing down the course twenty metres behind everyone else, faces like beetroots, legs like out-of-control stick insects, you will know why you are no good at athletics.

HOW TO SUCCEED ON SPORTS DAY

Here are a few tips to help you make the most of a horrible day...

Running Races - before the start, tie all the competitors' shoelaces together, cut the elastic holding their shorts up, or spread superglue on the soles of their shoes.

Long Distance Races - can easily be won if you hide after the start, wait until the bell for the last lap and rejoin the race when everyone else is clapped out.

For Cross-Country races - hide a mountain bike out on the track and sprint from the start, then jump on the bike and zoom for the finish line.

High Jump - tie a long piece of virtually invisible fishing line to the bar so you can pull it off every time someone else jumps. When it's your turn make sure you have placed a pair of springs in the heels of your shoes.

SPORTS DAY SUCCESS

More sure-fired sporting tips!

Long Jump - mix itching powder with the sand in the pit and make sure you go last - by this time everybody else will have retired, driven mad by the itching powder and you will win the competition by default.

Egg and Spoon Race - superglue your egg to the spoon or substitute your competitors' chicken eggs for ostrich eggs which will be too heavy to carry.

Shot Put - take a shot home and hollow it out with your dad's power drill; you will be able to throw it twice as far as anyone else. Alternatively, 'accidentally' drop your shot on the other competitors' toes - that should cramp their style!

Sack Race - before the race, knobble the other contenders by adding any of the following to their sacks; ants, grass snakes, hedgehogs, wasps, ferrets, carpet tacks or a pit bull terrier.

Obstacle Race - this is a fairly tame event as the obstacles are user-friendly things like plastic cones, tunnels, benches, rope-swings etc. Rather than take part you should help design the course, adding a few interesting extras like a water splash filled with piranhas, or quicksand sandpits, or exploding marker cones - if you also ensure that the obstacle race is the first event of the day, it should narrow the field of opposition for the other races.

CRICKET CAPERS

And now for the exciting game of cricket.
Rule number one - if you're playing
cricket, bring the right gear ...

Fielder - bring a camp bed, a nightshirt and
cap, your favourite teddy, some comics and
an alarm clock.

Settle yourself down for forty winks while
the opposition make 440 runs - the alarm
clock is to wake you up when it is your
turn to bat. If the ball comes your way
make sure you don't catch it - cricket balls
are very hard and will remove your fingers,
leaving you holding the stumps.

FOLLIES ON THE FIELD

Batsman - you will need a full set of armour, a bat one metre wide and a lucky charm, like a four-leaved clover or a rabbit's foot; if it doesn't want to lend you its foot, bring the whole rabbit – it's usually good for a few runs.

The technique for hitting a ball is simple; close your eyes, hold the bat well out in front of you and pray the bowler is a bad shot.

Bowler - you will need a pair of starting blocks, a spring-loaded arm, machine gun sights and a ball with the batsman's name on it. The rest is simple; just sprint from the blocks, line up the sights, release the arm and watch the ball knock the batsman's head off - with luck one of the fielders will catch it and he will be out for a dead duck.

Umpire - in order to qualify you must have been dead for at least two years and own a silly white hat. All you have to do is stand in one spot all day and pretend to be a coat hanger for all the players' jumpers and caps.

Wicket Keeper - bring a shovel, a large fishing net and a letter from your family doctor certifying that you are insane.

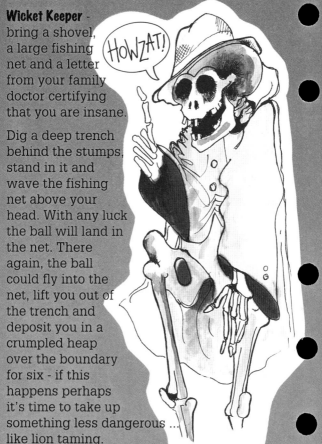

HOWZAT!

Dig a deep trench behind the stumps, stand in it and wave the fishing net above your head. With any luck the ball will land in the net. There again, the ball could fly into the net, lift you out of the trench and deposit you in a crumpled heap over the boundary for six - if this happens perhaps it's time to take up something less dangerous ... like lion taming.

Meanwhile, back at the Pavilion ...

Scoring - all you need for this is a scoreboard the size of a drive-in movie screen, and a six hundred page Basic Rules of Cricket manual. From time to time, just check that you have the scores wrong by at least twenty runs and three wickets as this is traditional.

Note: Your games teacher will only play in the school match if he is allowed to show off with his triple back somersault googly out-swinger ball which takes five minutes to hit the stumps after he has bowled it, makes the wicketkeeper dizzy, the umpire sick and spins three times round the batsman's ankles before jumping into the air and knocking out the middle stump – this is so boring for everybody else that you are advised to ban the delivery before the match begins; then the teacher will go into a huff and you can have a nice day without him.

DUMBBELLS

There are two types of dumbbells - the first kind are the big weights on each end of a bar that idiots lift to give them more muscles. These dumbbells are almost as boring as the people who use them.

Your P.E. teacher will show off by twizzling an enormous pair over his head and trying to look dead cool. This is known as the "'Hey, look, aren't I a brilliant guy?' Look". A feather under the armpit will sort him out. When he drops the dumbbells through the very expensive gym floor, watch him drop that smug expression, too.
Hmmm ... very satisfying.

"RA-RA-RA!!!"

The other type of dumbbell wears a ra-ra skirt, long hair tied in ribbons and has a huge powder-puff-type-thing growing at the end of each arm. No one knows why these dumbbells exist, or what they hope to achieve by standing on the sidelines at football matches singing really awful songs and flapping their powder-puff-type-things in the air - if you have any theories, please write to the Unidentified Dumbbells Research Institute as they are making a study of these peculiar creatures.

HORRIBLE HOCKEY

Hockey is a game of organised warfare where two teams are allowed to bash the legs off their opponents and launch a very hard ball at each others' heads. The game is started with something called a bully-off where the biggest bullies from each team meet in the middle and attack each other with sticks to see who is the toughest.

Goalkeepers wear 'Michelin Men' outfits and strap colanders to their heads to help with the strain of keeping the ball out of the net. The best way to avoid being injured is not to play (see Good Excuses).

Not so jolly Hockey Sticks on Ice
There is another version of the game called
ice hockey where great big brutes on
skates beat each other up whilst flying
round a rink at forty kilometres per hour.
Ice hockey is a spectator sport - which
means it's best enjoyed from a safe
distance outside the rink! This action
packed game is ideal for people with a
death wish - otherwise, don't be tempted!

FOOTBALL FLOPS

Football is a very popular sport with kids because you can always have a game with your friends in the street, the park or on the beach. Sports like Formula One motor racing or free-fall parachute jumping aren't so popular because your dad won't lend you his car and your mum doesn't want her best tablecloth used as a parachute.

If you're in the school football team, beware. You may have to play Useless Comprehensive, in the fifty-sixth division of the school's league.

Take a peek at their team sheet.

Central Defender - Mighty King Kong
The school's mascot and substitute headmaster. Kong is usually shown the red card within two minutes of the kick-off because he likes to bite opponents' legs.

Left Back -
Short O'Brains
Shorty, as he is affectionately known, is usually left back in the changing rooms where he can do no harm.

Right Back -
Cedric Wallflower
Cedric's hobbies are embroidery and basket weaving - perhaps that's why the manager calls him a basket case?

Sweeper - Mrs Rosy Cheeks
Mrs Cheeks (the school cleaner) likes to keep the pitch in tip top condition by trimming it with a pair of nail scissors during matches.

Goalkeeper - Jim Petunia
He doesn't like to stop the ball as he thinks that's what the net is for.

Midfield - Arty Phil Dodger and Oliver Twisted

These two are very good at controlling play on the centre spot but refuse to move off it in case they get lost.

It is quite easy to play round them.

Left Wing -
Streaky Smith
The fastest player in the country. Streaky can do the hundred metres in 1.6 seconds; he hasn't learned how to stop yet, so usually gets only one run per game which could last all afternoon - give him a wave on his way out of the stadium.

Right Wing -
John O'Goat
A difficult player with a very bad temper. John will spend most of the match beating up supporters in the stand and is usually arrested by the police before half-time.

Strikers - Ian Wrong and Bandy Cole

Ian's strength is in the air as he is very good at jumping and a bit of a head case, but if his first shot at the goal misses, he runs home to mummy in tears. Bandy Cole is very good at kicking the opposition but has never been known to actually kick the ball.

Useless United have been relegated from every division they have played in but their loyal fans still go wild if they manage to lose a game by less than forty goals. They did score once but nobody can remember how and it may be just another footballing legend.

HALF TIME SCORE 40 1 (OWN GOAL)

GORY GYMNASTICS

The school gym is a special kind of torture chamber, designed by teachers who want to get their own back. Funny thing is, some kids actually like it!

A session usually starts with warming up exercises. These tire you out before the real torture begins. The silliest of them is running on the spot where you have to run as fast as you can without actually going anywhere. Worthwhile...

This might be followed by tumbling and somersaults on the mat, which is alright if you happen to be a cat or have elastic bones.

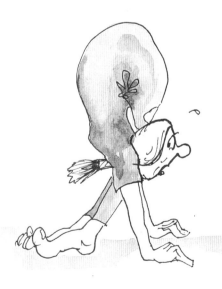

The most tricky exercise in the gym is vaulting. The name probably comes from re-volting, which is how you feel after you've done a bit of it...

You bounce off a springboard like a kamikaze swallow and do a series of complicated midair manoeuvres before landing perfectly back on your feet. Fat chance!

You will also be asked to do other fun things like climbing the wall bars, swinging from ropes and running along narrow beams - excellent training for any child planning to become a pirate when they leave school!

GOOD EXCUSES

Pleading illness or injury is the best possible way to get out of games. Remember, it has to be convincing or your hard-hearted teacher will just say, "Come on, the exercise will do you good."

Athlete's Foot - simply tell the teacher that your foot failed a drugs test and is banned from doing any sport for one year.

Tennis Elbow - cut a tennis ball in half, glue it on to your elbow and moan a lot.

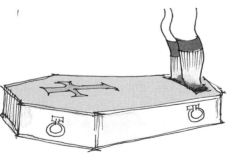

Dead Leg - this is a difficult but very effective one as it is hard to walk with a coffin strapped round your leg.

Common Cold - stick a strip of green slime to the end of each nostril and shiver like a nervous whippet.

Chicken Pox - stick your bottom and elbows out, stand on one leg, flap your arms and cluck like a demented hen.

Fractured Skull - wrap your head in bandages and splash tomato ketchup over them...it may not work as the teacher knows you haven't got a brain anyway.

German Measles - paint red spots all over your body and keep answering 'guten Morgen, mein Herr' when the teacher asks you a question.

A BAG OF TRICKS

Kit is the equipment you have to drag to school in your sports bag. Naturally the kit will vary depending on the sport you have been press-ganged into...

For **rugby** practice you will need things that make you look even more ugly than usual. Stick-on cauliflower ears, a big roll of black sticky tape to wrap round your head and a fluorescent gum shield in bright orange or green for that winning smile.

Footballers just need spare lipstick as it tends to wear off when kissing each other after scoring.

Tennis players need ten spare tennis racquets, a mirror to check that their hair is just right and a chest wig with attached gold chain and medallion.

Athletes need a range of figure-hugging lycra running outfits, preferably in colours that clash.

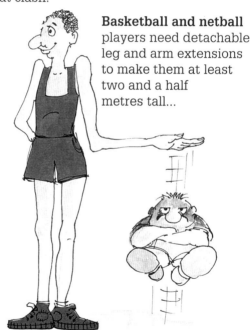

Basketball and netball players need detachable leg and arm extensions to make them at least two and a half metres tall...

...and **boxers** need satin shorts at least three sizes too big and a pair of horseshoes that fit neatly into their gloves.

BLOODSPORTS

Does he mean fox hunting? Don't be fooled - almost any sport is a bloodsport because P.E. and games teachers want you to give '100 percent'. So if you are carried off the games field, bleeding, on a stretcher, it's all part of the sport.

To these bloodthirsty teacher types, who lurk about gyms with tracksuits, whistles and very short haircuts, you are just ...

a Wimp - (That's any pupil who has sense enough to realise that charging around a pitch waving a stick, with a crowd of armed elephants thundering after you, or hanging upside down from a piece of string tied to a rafter, is downright dodgy.)

P.E. teachers don't like these pupils because they aren't eager to be 'part of the team' - P.E. teachers love teams so they can play referee and blow their silly whistles.

I'M OFF

Or you could be ...

a Sporty Type - (Misguided pupils who think it's all good fun to run themselves into the ground, perform death-defying stunts in the gym or give up their Saturday mornings to gallop around a muddy pitch, kicking a piece of leather while the opposition try to break their ankles.)

P.E. teachers like these pupils best.

HAVE A HEART, MISS!

Don't fret if you're hurt in the rough and tumble. P.E. teachers know just how to cope with ...

Cuts - despite the torrent of sticky red stuff pumping out of your shredded kneecap, you're told that it is only a graze, given a quick wipe down with a watery sponge and ordered back on the field.

Sprains - no one will believe that you have sprained your ankle so if you carry on limping you will be called a cissy and the rest of the team will be encouraged to ignore you.

Bruises - no sympathy here but, if it's big enough, and blue enough, the whole class will congratulate you on the size of your bruise.

WHAT A WHOPPA!

Bumps - these come in many sizes. If you have an egg-sized one, you will be told to stop making such a fuss. If you have a grapefruit-sized one, you will be told to leave the field, get it seen to and hurry back.

If you have a bump the size of a football, you will have passed out from shock/horror/amazement - when you wake up you will be in hospital surrounded by clucking nurses who will say something like "my, you have been in the wars"...you will be able to reply "no I haven't; we were just playing bloodsports in school today!"

BLAZING SADDLES

You won't have much chance at school to practise being a jockey unless your school happens to keep a stable of race horses in the playground. Instead you could practise on your mother's clothes horse, the school's vaulting horse or just get on your high horse and experience the thrills and spills of horse racing.

There are two important facts to remember if you want to become a jockey -

1 All jockeys are midgets and should weigh less than a bag of potatoes.

2 Horses are great, big, mean, bad-tempered things which always do the opposite of what you want them to do. Oh, yes, and they like nothing better than kicking you into next week or sinking their teeth into your delicate flesh.

There are two types of horse racing -

Flat Racing, where the horses gather in a friendly neighbour's flat and gallop round the furniture, and ...

National Hunt Racing, where the horses chase a foreign national (say a Frenchman or an Eskimo) over a series of jumps whilst trying to throw their jockeys into the nearest ditch.

BE A GOOD LOSER

The worst thing about sports is losing. Phrases like "May the best man win", or "It's only a game" don't help at all. Especially if you've just battled for forty minutes against a team of vicious demons in the freezing rain, and then lost the game.

It may seem odd, but you are supposed to congratulate the opposition; shake their hands and be all nice and chummy. All this after they've just run you into the ground, pulled your ears off, thrashed the life out of you, taught you a lesson, shown you how the game should be played AND given you a hiding.

Instead of saying "well played" to the rotten brute who has just beaten you, wouldn't you feel much better if you could roll about on the ground screaming blue murder? No? No, well maybe that's not quite right either. How about getting your big brother to beat him up after the match? Or hit him over the head with the huge silver cup he just won?

Now, wouldn't that make you feel a lot better?

Swimming is one of the most uncomfortable sports you will be made to do at school because ...

1 All your friends will get to see your pale, spotty body in its swimming costume and will laugh at your physique (or lack of it).

2 You are forced to walk through a revolting footbath filled with icy, smelly liquid that is designed to dissolve your feet.

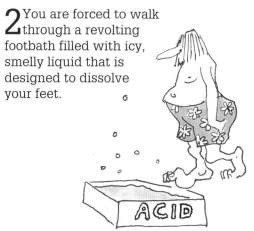

ACID

3 You are not a duck which means you are not designed for water. The first time you are told to dive in by your teacher, you will sink to the bottom of the pool like a stone and sit there with a surprised look on your face. Quack, quack.

4 If you accidentally swallow some water, it's best not to think about the germs, bugs and microbes of at least five hundred other children who used that water just before you. Gulp!

5 If you enter races you will have to wear a pair of really silly looking goggles and one of those skintight caps - this means you will look like a bald frog with bad eyesight.

6 When you are floating calmly on your back thinking nice thoughts, extremely fat kids with a warped sense of humour will jump on you from the side of the pool and try to drown you.

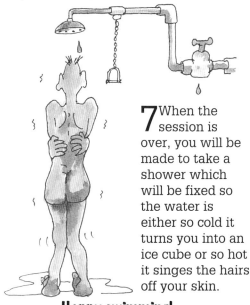

7 When the session is over, you will be made to take a shower which will be fixed so the water is either so cold it turns you into an ice cube or so hot it singes the hairs off your skin.

Happy swimming!

All sports freaks love statistics. They're always delighted to tell you such important things as who was the reserve goalkeeper for Bloodbank United in the 1857 Cup Final.

Here are a few vital statistics you might like to quote back at them. With luck it will shut them up!

▪ The world endurance record for playing with a Yo-yo is 8 hours 7 minutes 13 seconds - and that is an awful lot of ups and downs!

▪ The greatest distance achieved in a national spitting competition is 24 feet 10 inches - do not try this at home!

▪ The duration record for see-sawing is 115 hours 33 minutes, and what sore bottoms they must have had!

- In 1968, Zolilio Diaz rolled a hoop 600 miles in 18 days - what an idiot!

- The longest game of hopscotch on record lasted 26 hours and ended because the players went hopping mad.

- The marathon record for an egg and spoon race is 20 miles in 5 hours 25 minutes - why?

- The record distance for throwing a rolling pin is 138 feet 11 inches by Sheri Salyer - not the sort of person you would want as your mother!

- The longest continuous shower was taken by a Mr Peter Schell and lasted for 168 hours by which time he was able to show the spectators a clean pair of heels!

DAFT DEFINITIONS

The SAS Guide to the origins of sport...

Table Tennis - a game invented by two Chinese men, Mr Ping and Mr Pong, who were batty about tennis but lived too far away to go to Wimbledon.

Discus - this was invented by D.J.s as a way of getting rid of unwanted records.

Pole Vault - This sport doesn't come from Poland, as you might expect, but from Outer Mongolia instead. In Mongolia there are so many mountains that the locals used to spend all day just walking up and down valleys. Then someone invented the pole vault. Now everyone carries a long twangy stick to project themselves from one hillside to the next. It saves time, so they do it as their national pastime, too.

Kart Racing - this began in Ye Olde Merry England when bad King John issued an edict banning people from putting the horse before the cart, so people pulled the carts instead and had races to see who was quickest.

Boxing - began in ancient Japan as a branch of the gentle art of origami or paper folding, where people competed to see how quickly they could make a box from an ordinary sheet of paper. Unfortunately the contestants began to fight with each other and were soon throwing punches instead of making boxes.

American Football - this is an idiot's version of soccer combined with rugby, for big powder puffs padded up with mattresses and motor bike helmets in case they accidentally hurt each other.

Football - originally a board game called Subbuteo which the human players copied by hopping round the field on huge upturned mushrooms. The goalies were tied to the end of telegraph poles and were moved about by the crowd.

Rugby - this was invented as a type of tribal warfare in ancient Britain; the idea was to kill as many of the opposing team as possible in eighty minutes. It hasn't changed to this day.

Synchronised Swimming - no one knows who invented this sport or why. It is performed by Barbie dolls with clothes pegs stuck to their noses and is extremely weird.

Water Polo - first recorded game was by members of the Trumpton Leisure Centre Mixed Bathers Association on the 3rd February, 1897, when Mr Alf Butterfingers dropped a well known mint into the swimming pool and two hundred volunteers tried to find it for him.

GAME FOR A LAUGH

Some ancient and very odd sports you may like to play with your friends:

Hopscotch -
an excellent game for the playground; everybody hops about on one leg shouting 'hoots aye, the noo mon' at the tops of their voices. The winner is the last one to be caught by the teacher when the bell goes for afternoon lessons.

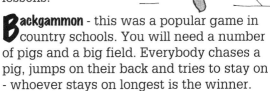

Backgammon - this was a popular game in country schools. You will need a number of pigs and a big field. Everybody chases a pig, jumps on their back and tries to stay on - whoever stays on longest is the winner.

Jacks - a fun game for lunch time. While the teachers are stuffing themselves in the staffroom, everybody sneaks out to the car park, jacks up the teachers' cars and removes the wheels - the winner is the person who removes most wheels in the time available.

Hide and Seek - best kept for really boring lessons; when the teacher's back is turned everybody sneaks out of the room as quietly as possible and finds a hiding place. The winner is the person who isn't discovered until the end of school.

Blow Football - another excellent playground game; each player must have a vacuum cleaner on a long lead. Set the vacuum cleaners to blow instead of suck and use them to blow the football around the playground trying to score goals.

GETTING YOUR OWN BACK

Since your teacher is going to force you to take part in horrible sporting activities it is only fair that you get your own back...try some of the following:

- Stick a wheel clamp to teacher's feet and use him as a rounders' base.

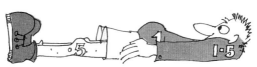

- Paint measurements up his arms and legs, and lie him beside the long jump pit.

- Still with feet and inches painted up his body, tie a string to his feet and dangle him in the swimming pool - he'll make the ideal depth and temperature gauge. (If he goes blue, the water is definitely too cold for swimming; there again, it could be lack of air...oops!)

101 OTHER USES FOR A GAMES TEACHER

(... well, 4 really...)

- Walk him by the ankles, on his hands, around the pitch. Put a white paintbrush in his mouth and he can paint the lines beautifully.

- Sit him in a cardboard box on the obstacle race course - then he will find out that colliding with an obstacle hurts!

- In the sack race, put the bag over his head instead of his feet, and point him in the direction of the next town.

- When he sends you on a cross country run on a cold, snowy day, tell the class to swap the route. All detour back to school another way, leaving teacher freezing on the spot, stopwatch in hand, for hours!

Since you are going to have to play sports at school anyway, you might as well enjoy them...so put on a brave smile and take a leaf out of Arthur Letics well known book:

There's Nothing So Funny as a Sporting Bunny

Who is the fastest rabbit of all time over 100 metres?

Bugs Runny

What do you call a fish that's good at motor sport?

Damon Brill

Who is the fastest fish of all time over 100 metres?

Finford Christie

Who is the funniest jockey of all time?

Jester Piggot

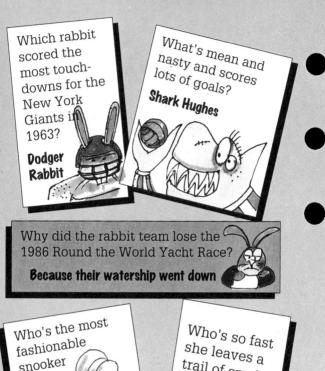

Which rabbit scored the most touch-downs for the New York Giants in 1963?

Dodger Rabbit

What's mean and nasty and scores lots of goals?

Shark Hughes

Why did the rabbit team lose the 1986 Round the World Yacht Race?

Because their watership went down

Who's the most fashionable snooker player?

Stephen Trendy

Who's so fast she leaves a trail of smoke behind her?

Sally Funnel

Who's the fastest runner in history?

Adam (because he was first in the human race)